NOT IN MY OWN LAND

Poems by

MATTHEW McDIARMID

ABERDEEN UNIVERSITY PRESS

First published 1984
ABERDEEN UNIVERSITY PRESS
A member of the Pergamon Group

© Matthew McDiarmid 1984

British Library Cataloguing in Publication Data

McDiarmid, Matthew
    Not in my own land
    I. Title
    821'914   PR6025.A217/
    ISBN 0—08—030404—4 (Pbk)

Printed in Great Britain
The University Press
Aberdeen

INDEX OF FIRST LINES

A minstrel from the ever twisting ways
he'd pick a tune,
finger it a little, and quite soon
you'd have a song the morning had not known
but afternoon was singing everywhere,
something forgotten in the world
and lost with so much beauty that till then
had only waited for remembering.
A poet of Provence,
but it was you I thought of, how the smile
came to your lips like morning, how it played
upon them till the sun filled all the sky
and the new time
always and everywhere was afternoon.

—ooOoo—

The rain came endlessly
that endless afternoon
when we went wondering endlessly
that time should stay for us.
The ungainly graceful bears
swung endlessly as one
and the crowd's steadied stares
swung with them endlessly;
endlessly penguins posed
and endlessly amused;
in light-dimmed tanks shapes swirled
and momentarily stilled
endlessly stared.
Around us children endlessly
played their unending game,
scenes changed, changed endlessly
and each one was the same,
you with your dark dank hair
trailing a dream-white face,
half-smiling that my gaze
followed you endlessly.

—ooOoo—

1

This is the spring, with blood unreconciled,
ardourous, insolent, unqualified;
vagrant in town as country her desires
sharp from the winter garish walk the streets.
She fans the winds with smouldering fumes of lusts,
her longings flower in park and window-box,
these are her dreams that flee before the crowd,
her impulse in the ever hurrying feet.
She brings renewal of forgotten graces,
the winter's dignities look shabby now,
and in the windowed arcades women walk
designing personalities anew.
This is the spring, no flower-girl pale of hue
vending a faded beauty from shy stalls,
she is a Spanish dancer bold of grace
tossing a rose of passion from her lips.
She has not the slow languors of the summer,
the somnolence of August afternoons,
she is awake in each daemonic step,
her castanets ring clear across the streets
and near and cruel comes their invitation.
If she would only stop, the dance be done,
if I could come at her and make her mine,
but the mad round goes on, the dancer mocks,
there is no heart in her, only a flame.
She is the crowd clamant in every colour,
clamant as April skies of clouds so clear,
she is the spring that never loved a lover,
whose only thought is of the earth's increase.
Dance and mock on, it may be with the summer
she will regret the girl that was the spring,
or not regret, whom love pursued a season
and whom my year will never see again.

—ooOoo—

The tree peeled to a winter's black and white
raked the bare sky. Above the brae of stumps
it swung so free, my coloured skeleton,
not just another tree, for in my mind
it kept its morning magic, green and wet
and personal as when I saw it stand

2

alone against the colours of the dawn,
outliving them. But you were with me then.
Trees are mysterious, they have their lives.
I never could have caught its secret growth,
the inmost stealth of its most still existence,
but vision is more simple; what we see
is meaning, and I saw what you had meant,
against the death-scarred hill the thrust of life
seeking all it can ever seek or find,
a language.

—ooOoo—

I was playing in a forest,
not so dark but the sun came through;
I think my mother was with me, and other
children; we played as children do.

I was running beside the forest,
there were houses, some two or three,
sometimes I ran into the forest
but there was less and less to see.

There was a town and now the forest
was dwindled down to the wood I knew
but it still held sunshine, saw the sky,
and often I walked in it with you.

There was nor forest nor wood, just houses,
and we had one, we liked it well;
windows still showed the sun, and inside
to make more sunshine we worked a spell.

We hardly noticed at first the sunshine
was growing less and we'd lost the spell,
but we thought more and more of the great forest
as it had stood before it fell.

We were out of the sky and sunshine
in a tunnel that turned and turned again
and it seemed to us that the endless tunnel
cried out and shook for the coming train.

Darkness, but a light glinting through it
we saw at last, the light came on.
Incredibly there were birds, trees, sunshine
and an incredibly shouting dawn.

The dawn rose, it had risen for others,
we were content just that it shone
and that so many of these others
walked in the forest that was gone.

They walked as if the world were empty
and life were to begin anew,
and in their dream the wood was endless
as when I walked in it with you.

—ooOoo—

A poet lucky in one verse
and this not all his making, he
found Richard and his moment came,
Gaillard and everyone's dead king;
not the best singer but that once
he sang 'O Richart, o mon roi',
and there was all love's tenderness
in the small graces of his song.

—ooOoo—

'The gentle rose spiritual and bland
dreams on its own sufficient loveliness,
a pulse of beauty summer's tending hand
feels beat with every moment less and less;

yet time is justified in that flushed cheek,
and death here shows his subtle gardening
so to make beauty brief, and so to seek
the flower of spirit in no stronger thing'.

Written of roses when the world was young
and in the garden voices played and played,
and were called in, and still the night air rung,
and day had been the harmony they made;

but now the walks are silent where they sped,
the flowers hang foolish, time has left his game,
the night hours hold the rose too dearly dead
and day goes thinking on the uncalled name.

—ooOoo—

Ravened beneath night's cliff the beast
and leaping clawed its upward way,
there to be killed. The cave approved,
along its shining way it too would kill.

The givers were long gone, the gift
recalled their kindness but of late
he'd wondered at the choice. They had
gone shopping and it seemed to wait

their purchasing; shadows took shape,
voluble hands above it went,
a bargain not to be refused.
They'd bought it, as it always meant;

bought silence rich upon a floor,
and patterning such as a home
should have and give, its centring paths
the only ones it let thought roam.

Now at day's quiet end he knew
that patterning for his. It talked
with him in the loud nights and still
of its remembering; when walked

the far-come strangers through his dream
who were not of his time, and when
far-sent the night-come visions came
of the first making, strangest then

even for time's latest citizen.
The high-rise, floating like an ark
above its sea of moving lights,
looked past them to the houseless dark

and there each winding glittering stream.
The shining shaken face below
looked back at him, against the night
its features seemed to change and flow.

The firth was an exploring thought
with ends of darkness, and the hills
imaginings; there would be pools
and hollows where heard silence spills

from listening trees, a world not his,
the outlines only just made out
by deeper dark and the few lights
that signalled wilderness about.

Something out there was wandering
that felt no impulse to come in,
and knew him from before this room;
that never would have wished to win

here to his peace and patterning
but wander farther, something shy
of cities. Then it was he saw
the light had changed in the room's sky.

Before him in the seated dark
the carpet glimmered, the bright floor
stretched from fantastic wall to wall,
lighted and lightening the more.

Woven long before his time, he'd glimpsed
the shuttles flying in his room,
and heard, or so it seemed to him,
the threading hurry of the loom.

Nights he had sat entranced with it,
the lines that hither-thither fled,
and the blue glow that fled with them,
and central the great core of red,

the core of red that pulsed and glowed.
Almost a fire, a life apart
seemed burning there; the lines were veins
feeding an incandescent heart.

And now into the room was come
fear as a creature fully grown,
and visible, and it had eyes
and they were fixed on him alone.

And the nights passed, the nights that brought
the wished as unwished images;
it was a gentle beast that held
strange power and stranger will to please,

but the nights passed, new visions came;
not only carpet, ceiling, wall,
were large and vital presences
above him in the room so small.

Once there had been residual quiet,
a peace imagined on the firth
and in the hills receding still
and ever reassuring earth,

and trees that thought. Alone was left
all that he'd ever had, his room,
and from its shadowed depths the light
that spoke the working of the loom,

the shuttles flying as they'd been
even when the hands above it went
and the kind givers thought they chose.
This had been always what was meant,

the cave that killed. He would have laughed
but a sure sense of things come near
took him, tension not all his own,
and the red carpet fixed his fear.

On his last night he heard quite clear
a singing as of too taut wire,
and the electric patterns glowed,
and the red heart burst into fire.

The chair he sat in held him tight,
the walls were falling, with the door;
it had grown quiet now and dark,
what was it lay there on the floor?

Now he could see himself, quite still,
at ease, the patterns through him ran.
The city entering from the night
looked down on its demolished man.

—ooOoo—

I must have lain with a strange woman
and not in my own land,
and looked on a far country
not mine to understand
and yet it haunted me.
I must have caught words of her language
spoken into some marvellous night
when the moon was at brightest and fullest
and I heard and spoke them aright.
I must have run for her many errands
into the market-place
and sat with the tall dark strangers,
the men of another race
whose customs were happiness.
I must have walked through hot afternoons
in the blind-white streets alone,
sensing past shadowed doorways
a life that was not my own
and never could be my own.
I must have cried out in some night-hour
not knowing what things I said,
and wakened to a bright morning
and a smile that comforted,
where nothing was to be said.
I must have gone with a wise-sad company
to some point of their vanishing skies
where I stopped to look back on her city
and heard them say their goodbyes,
and they made me not to remember
and took from me all but desire.

What she was, how she looked, that woman
I knew past the shadow-line,
is lost to me but her country
will always almost be mine.

—ooOoo—

At Sunium where the sky went higher,
its one lone cloud more lonely at that height,
and landward hill on hill such distance flying
in such pure light,
we knew the miracle of grace
movement can be,
felt we had glimpsed the opening of hands
and the release of beauty on the air.
About the brilliant column,
along its unimaginable floor
the bright bird sped; it rose
to find its home in that light element,
itself more light, and when it fell
white wings still went about the column
and did not cease.
Were there vendors of old wares
raucous on the time-worn steps,
loud strangers summer-garmented?
There may have been;
all sounds other now are fled
but the steady beat of wings,
the bright encompassing.

—ooOoo—

I have awakened shadows, given them tongue,
listening among them in an ancient room
where they still lengthened with the afternoon
and touched the vase and the boy handling it.
Blue, dark and delicate, to him it meant
a mystery of China, quaint, remote,
something quite precious and quite rare,
and that could break.

I listen now and effortlessly hear
the summons of that gong-stroke sent so clear
across the silence of the lake
to where the harmonious lovers meet,
and the faint brush-stroke of a bridge
above dark waters does not separate
such looking loves. I wait,
with each reverberation sure to see
the admonitory crack
and a world disappear,
the lovers on the bridge, the willowtree,
and wonder it should last.

—ooOoo—

Being in bed with you
so I began to dream,
gates opened and shut,
time was a singing stream.

We moved through a city
of one street without end,
lights came on in the city
that seemed so much a friend.

I turned to speak to you,
I could not see your face,
you were so many people,
I loved you in that place.

You took me to you
in silence no word broke,
fierce love and pity
not meant for us awoke.

Loving you my lips brushed
symbols and signs, not you,
worlds that I did not know
moved under me and spoke;

and as they spoke no city
was there, no lights, no folk,
I saw you, and that moment
you went and I awoke.

10

Along the singing river
the way of coloured lights
led me to you waiting
after many nights.

—ooOoo—

I have seen young women
with careful questing hands
sort through odd bits of cloth
as if they chose their dreams.
and it may be one was Helen,
another was Eurydice,
and all time's lovely women
were shopping in that store.

Penelope, Ariadne,
Cressid, Thais, Penthesile,
Lucrezia, Marcia, Messalin,
Bathsheba, Rachel, Ruth,
Iseult, Francesca, Nicolette,
the Marys, Stewart and Morrison,
were come to hunt for beauty
and went from floor to floor.

Their men went with them patiently,
almost it seemed unseeingly,
they might have been mere clockwork
moving to hidden springs,
but in their eyes was Jason
journeying with his Argonauts
and if they'd found Medea
it was on Colchis' shore.

Always there were assistants,
smiling department managers;
I saw one bow to Helen
as if he praised her choice.
But in another city
and in another country
the Master of the Fashions
had chosen the dreams they wore.

And both the men and women
that wandered between counters
were suddenly time's children
and lost and seeking home;
the aisles they walked were deserts,
and full of giants and ogres,
and for the spell upon them
they wandered evermore.

—ooOoo—

My cousin in her cottage by the firth
told me how with the winter the deer came
into the garden, and from bush and rose
stripped stalk and leaf, at last moved driftingly
back to their hungry snows; their antlered heads
like firm antennae trained to the one call
found north, entered and surged for home;
she fancied some fast height, some rock-rimmed cache
heathered and mossed, some place of last resort
out of the worst of winds the few would reach.
My thought was on the need that stripped a rose
(here the red rose blooms late), against the snow
kindlings of colour, scatterings of scent.

—ooOoo—

I remember folly and how our looks once met,
who was slow and dark and suddenly alight,
who would say no deliberately as descends the night
and yes tumultously as the mouth-red dawn,
who was always folly;
whose hair is yet a memory in these hands
and for its auburn lights,
whose smile I heard clearer than all her words,
whose voice talks on.
So much else is forgotten, folly I would not forget.

—ooOoo—

Death in the desert's always bright,
bones whiten, the abandoned truck
signals into the sun, gunned tanks
shine still though canted odd degrees
where life ran out; debris, yet all
reflects as life, most simple here
and brilliant. Tented morning sees
emptiness filling up with light,
and past hushed dunes, just visible
through veils of heat the misted blue
of mountains, peak by unseen peak
caught in the gradual train of fire.
The order of expected day
quietly as splendidly begins:
morning slow rising to its noon
of sufferance, by afternoon
insufferably prolonged; at length
the first drawn sigh of night's relief
and evening entering with stars,
predictably the unclouded moon
with full effect of vast surprise.
Nowhere is life so simply one
or set in so intense a scene.
Beauty by bare existence shows
more beautiful: a rocky ledge
sending its flash of flowers alone,
a dusty thornbush not quite grey
and a scarred wahdi almost green,
brave shoots of growth that front a sky
blind in its blue infinity,
its line most beautiful of all.
Sometimes day's glitter softens, ghosts,
the desert dreams, dreams skies and sands,
and walking through its dream is seen
a shape imagined as a man
khaftaned and sandalled, for his home
if anywhere on earth is here,
yet looking nowhere, for the dream
and all its endless scenery
are his.

—ooOoo—

The skies fell, all of a wild night
the wahdi raged, with the daylight
were only tracks of a spent tide
soon sun and shifting sands would hide.
Nothing had happened, that wild scene
was stilled as it had never been,
no roiling wave of racing life,
no rocks that felt the slap and strife
of waters; the great rain had made
its bid for freedom, seen it stayed
and foiled in wastes. And I could think,
seeing the torrent drain and shrink,
no other of the dead I'd known,
sticks crossed and helmeted, alone
where the wind blew unsparingly
and made of sticks and helmet play.
They too had channelled a full life
of racing hopes and tides of strife,
they too were tideless now and bare
and the great waters flowed elsewhere,
they too had perished in the plains
and dreamt the secret day of rains.

—ooOoo—

I heard their beggarly chant
and felt the hate unquenchable
seethe in that forest of stone,
and for all that no leaves there worried,
no sough, no chatter, no song,
there were words in the air that crackled and burst
like a deadly rifle fire.
Always a change of hates troubled the forest,
change that was still the same.
Beyond it was the desert, full of life
after that bitter wood, and the great sun
singing with killing heat; and men,
not hating but with ever hardening heart,
their passions as petrescent as once were
the waters where these twisted trunks took shape
through whitening aeons.

Nothing was changed, nothing went anywhere.
The hard stones dreamed all day
in a white, a shining stupour,
the grey sands shuffled and fell
and had not moved at all.

—ooOoo—

'I would the windmill and the wind
were ceased and the mill's arms,
and nevermore again I'll see
their sorceries and charms,
but what I know is that the wind
goes blowing evermore
and on this loneliest road in Spain
I see them still before.

I would the wind were fallen away
to such a dead and calm
that nothing moved for nothing lived
to mouth this mad "I am";
for when I most lived then I dreamed
so absolute a dream
that nothing after comes so real
as that which only seemed:

with mangy horse, an antique lance,
as antique shield and plate,
and on a donkey blithe beside
a clown for fitting mate,
a crazy elf-locked knight rides forth
past gawking fields of Spain
to win a kingdom and content
he will not know again'.

—ooOoo—

When he most wanted him his father was not there,
the women were, but all their hungry care
was for his body; when it all was done
they would demand it. Then he knew despair
but in his cry he was his father's son.
They claimed it, found that it was gone,
it had to come again.

—ooOoo—

A whir and creak of strange machinery,
the iron shadows sleeping by St Mark's
rouse to their customed task. Venice looks up.
Precise the hour-door opens and comes forth
the angel trumpeter of the good news,
next the three Magi journeying to adore
God and God's mother wheeling still before —
Isis with doomed Osiris at her breast,
Venus with pouting Cupid, what you will.
Last in the punctual circle railed and grooved
two Moors with hammers lofted, infidel,
send their dismissive stroke. Paraded faiths
suffer their spasm in darkness and are still;
and in the little liberty of the great square
the doves that wheeled in lovely senseless flight
fall to their peck again. Venice resumes.

—ooOoo—

Un mazzolin de' fiori
che vien' dalla campagn'

Flowers have a life in stillness
and a persisting grace,
and such a life in stillness
was in my flower-girl's face.

Daily at the same stand
she made her offering,
and 'fine flowers from the country'
was all I heard her sing.

16

The white hands held their bouquet
as if her thoughts were flowers
blessed in some secret garden
with still refreshing showers.

The quiet gaze went by them,
the city passed unseen,
and absent from her business
she walked where they had been.

From her composed demeanor
and tranquil attitude
the streets might have been fields,
the flowers plucked where she stood.

The violets drooped and sickened
in the hot air of Rome
but she with all her being
stayed fresh and cool at home.

—ooOoo—

We came into a park where the sun shone
forever, and where people surely knew
one afternoon would follow like another
and the folk still be there for whom it shone,
as then it did for us until we slept.
The knowledge still was with us when we woke
in a green theatre. Its empty stage
would soon be filled, for waiting in the wings
were many characters, all stereotypes
and all set to be happy. Comedy
was what the day had written. We looked on,
knowing them idling actors on a set
whose stars were yet to come, and unconcerned
what play was picked, it would be of the park
and please. And still there was no happening.
Yet all around us running was the sound
of secret laughter, an enjoying crowd
at one in understanding of the theme,
how nothing, nothing changes after all,
or youth or age the plots were few and fixed.

But now the stars were come, somehow were come
unnoticed, to enact the endless scene
all others followed. Time for us stood still.
Adam and Eve were standing by a pool
and smiling so their image smiled again.
Or should have done; the pool smiled not at all,
a wind was on the water, then a cloud,
and next a rain like none was ever seen.
The day had chosen the wrong plot, and from
both park and play the actors unprepared
and streaming everywhere found no escape.

—ooOoo—

If I had been stupid Noah
I would have picked suicide.
What covenant should he have kept,
what hope was there in us?
I would have said
'Let it rain and rain and rain
so nothing of me or mine
come to dry land again'.
I would have drowned.
Thank God for stupid Noah with the hammer hands
who worked on his house of life,
who knocked up a boat to sail and sail and sail,
who sent forth birds.
Will there ever be a keeper of the kinds
so simple and so true as Noah was
with his two hammer hands?
Calvary makes less sense than Ararat.

—ooOoo—

Long heats of afternoon,
a distant unreal fisher
motionless by his pool;
on the thin atmosphere
across the sultry heather
blow wisps of too sweet perfume,

impulses of hot breath
from the thunder-ripe September;
the uneasy hill-side lists
into the exhausted air.
A boy pressing the turf
with vacant head on hands
sees nothing of the plain
that lies in rich suspense,
but follows absently
slow fumes of smouldering skies.
The lazy afternoon
is whistling to itself.
A tune, a meaning? No,
and yet the sound is there,
the scene, and all it wants
is noticing.

—ooOoo—

We watched it in the trees and in the grass
weave in and out the breathless shadow races,
tease their set beauty from the daffodils,
course the one cloud in a bewildering blue,
happiness, it ran there, ran everywhere.
Across the park it vaulted, a great clown,
its folly an infection on the wind
and veering as the dive and soar of kites;
raced till the day slowed warm and westering,
when happily it threw itself to ground.
So close we watched each movement and each mood
that if it had a thought that too was ours,
and all our thoughts were children. We had run
too fast to let our feelings overtake,
but now they did and happiness grew up.

—ooOoo—

I have seen stillness moving through my dream
like a loved person, but she would not stay,
and I have seen her when she naked lay
into my arms and then it was no dream,
and when she went she did not go away;

for still above my arm the bright head bent,
and the bare breasts above my bare breast leant
in the slow rhythm of sleep, so beautiful
not the dressed day could ever hope to seem.
Between her lips the breath so gently broke,
the still face trusted and was any child,
and so much more, that once again her fool
I had to kiss her so she half awoke
and stillness beyond stillness sleeping smiled.

—ooOoo—

Paris is like no other city,
names keep their magic when words fail.
They were seas we voyaged on,
beauty with no diminishing sail;
the green wave broke on your white body,
spring came to Paris like a gale,
and, the gale spent, the sleeping Paris
under my lips was kissing-pale.

Paris they say is like a woman
and always the imagined one,
who rises from your arms with morning
to enter with the set of sun,
that loveliest time of quiet Paris
when cars and metro cease to run
and the shared secret of a smile
says that the night is just begun.

Paris makes love, sometimes she loves,
and when she does all moments are
lonely that are not loving. We
laughed in the Brasserie Balzar,
and sang with Appia, and we knew
happiness always leaves a scar.
How else should we know happiness
had once been not so very far?

Paris is just like any city
and you like any woman too,
it just so happens that my Paris
among all women must be you,

and there can be no other city
tressed with a sunset of such hue
as has your hair, so that I touch it,
or almost think now that I do.

—ooOoo—

Heartbreak is a name, a town,
in it the streets go up and down,
I walk them. Falls the green green gown
still from you, Barbara?

Out of my world your face is gone
and still I see it in the dawn,
and the kissed lips my kiss stays on,
Barbara.

And when I ask the reason why
no one will answer, I could die,
but men are fools and do not cry,
do they Barbara?

The ache, the pain, have passed away
or so I tell myself each day
and night, but they have come to stay
for you, my Barbara.

The afternoons, they grow so long,
or is it time itself goes wrong?
Did my arms hold you like a song,
my Barbara?

You have the unforgotten face,
I feel your kiss like holy grace,
with you alone I find my place,
my Barbara.

When will the months turn into days,
the days to minutes, time that stays
still in the stillness of embrace,
Barbara?

—ooOoo—

I visited your cottage yesterday
and I could see that you were gone away.
It looked quite different without your care,
I knew and yet I did not know the place.
It might have noticed me was how I felt
but its attention seemed to be elsewhere;
I had imagined somehow it would talk.
The windows that looked outward now looked in,
the house was all itself and very still,
as were the trees along the gravelled walk;
the cypresses pursued their many thoughts
to ends none of our own. What had I hoped,
the green door opening to show you there,
the talk and tread of life upon the stair?
But there was nothing here. The white walls so
significant and knowingly discreet
were merely innocent. I came away,
and the companion strangeness of the street
came with me, others as directionless
and walking with like pace into the past
out of the future where so late they'd lived.
I should have known that this was how time moved.

—ooOoo—

Lady whose fingers drew
threads dark with light and knew
huntsman with hunted,
when the wind swept your hall,
troubled the bright-hung wall,
did you too hear the call
I hear so clearly?

Did the trees stand less still
along the wind-moved hill,
birds rise up crying,
the sounding charge sweep close
as the loud canvas rose,
and your own wise repose
did it too suffer?

I like to think you saw
sudden the hunter draw
bugle to lips and blow
death on the silence,
heard his harsh song as well,
felt all its ruthless spell,
its truth and torment.

'Time with a fell desire,
his lips and eyes afire,
breathes on the neck of life;
day pursues tiring day,
pleasure's a scarlet prey.
Up heart and ride away,
and no cares follow!

'An hour for love's excess,
beauty to wear its dress
and be its loveliest;
joy that would still be joy
must its own life destroy,
for Helen a burned Troy.
Up falcon, fetch her!

'When the green woods are still,
no more you make your kill
to the loud halloo,
when past's your wild career
and the sole horn you hear
is that yourself must fear,
winding so lonely,
think that you hunted well
ere you were hunted.'

That's what the hunter said
whose bugle notes are fled
I still hear sounding.
Still in time's forest they
challenge the dear-won prey,
still ring out harsh and gay,
'Kill and be killed'.

—ooOoo—

In the green twilight
I put my questions three
to her who sits and listens
beneath the dreaming tree.

'What things are good?'
She smiles and will not answer,
with haunted ear she lists
to the impudent romancer.

'What things are true?'
The questioner's forgot
and still she listens to the wind
and dreams of what is not.

'What things are divine?'
And now she seems to sigh,
all this foolish asking
for a fool's reply.

And listening so I left her,
that folly-haunted queen
who put aside my questions
as if they had not been.

In the green twilight
the spirit goes alone
in a silence singing
and a world her own.

—ooOoo—

The blood that flows through April's veins
has yet to splash May's dreaming cheeks
with rose and poppy from the lanes
yet that will come which no flower seeks.

Spring with soft process still aspires
invisibly as visibly,
and from its green and living fires
shoots tongues of wildest prophecy.

Life mindless, beautiful, on wing,
building to breed its beauty new
in bush and tree seeks the one thing
life for a season must pursue.

And yet how alien is this scene
of cold as bright automatism;
in the church militant of green
love is an ineffectual schism.

Still it relives the buried grief,
is silent when all else would sing,
and timelessly the fallen leaf
sees falling, even while it is spring.

—ooOoo—

'A rose for every season', summer said,
when there were clouds, such little, little clouds,
but winter came and struck the red rose dead,
and the blood seeping through its many shrouds
would not be staunched, no more my thoughts for you
to whom all seasons come now just the same.
Where you are gone the flowers are always few,
only a silence grows about your name.

—ooOoo—

How is the street where you are living,
houses two sides, and windows too,
doors with the usual colours giving
entrance and exit? Is it true
people live in them, and all find
the customary things to do?

Is there a traffic, cars and vans
such as the other cities know,
people on pavements who have plans
for this and that, places to go;
and with the dusk in the grey city
do the shapes slacken, seem to flow?

And with the night do lights come on
in lamps and windows, lone cars spear
the dark with brightness and soon gone
does the left quietness come more near?
Is there a time street voices fade
and only lamps and stars burn clear?

Do people go to bed, do some
know the one kindness, just to sleep,
some sleepless wait for day to come,
yet others love, the many keep
a dreaming tally of their days
till the free hours come by and steep

them in a bright oblivion?
Is this how things go in your town,
dawn shouting after shouting dawn:
'Get up, get out, go home, lie down,
make love, have children, love them, die',
and 'Don't you know your sergeant, Brown'?

Does all this happen in your street,
is all so strangely commonplace,
the day, the night, the scene complete,
the loving and the unloved face?
Is there an angry hurt so keen
it kills itself, is this the case?

And children's laughter when they run,
of all heard sounds the loveliest,
still heard as running when it's done --
Puer nobis datus est,
and taken away — does it run yet,
or is the running sound at rest?

And in your else so silent city
is there a noise of talking dreams,
all of them touching themes of pity,
and of the city's self it seems
as having no particular source
more than the sound of many streams?

One of such dreams how two came near
a beauty passing hope or thought
and made it theirs before the mere
process of living was their lot.
Such busy shadows, so unreal!
When was it that we last forgot?

—ooOoo—

They could have been and no way were absurd,
the handed pair in the small country church
where the light lengthened with them every day
and shortened, but the handclasp was the same
so patient bond, the same that they had meant.
Time that will sculpt with such exacting care,
character with so clean a cutting stroke
its speaking subjects,
and as decidedly deface its thoughts,
blur its best meanings, left theirs clear.
A man, his wife, five centuries had seen
them and their angels share
one attitude of prayer,
still to be so together, still maintain
the dogma of their endless matrimony,
two of the faithful dead.
Let them lie still together, still pretend
their ever valid sacrament,
the kingdom is not yet.

—ooOoo—

Coming and going betwixt the sun and the shade
the birds see only the track that the seasons have made,
and their singing is to the nest. Wings overhead
continuously, passing on their far business,
might have expressed the traffic of our loves
once but no more.

—ooOoo—

'Listen to me in the silence,
listen to me in the shade
by whom the heart's forest
continually is swayed.

I am the wraith of beauty
and we walk side by side,
sisters, but I the lovelier
in the pale eventide.

Seek for me by the fountains
or by the waterfalls
or rivulets of autumn
down which the bittern calls.

Surprise me by the sighing shore
of a low tide, fallen wind,
where day's full strength is running out
in shallows of spent mind.

Suffer me by the wood's edge
on which the late sun sets
and be at peace with sorrows
and dulcet-toned regrets.

I am the wish for children
that must stay unbegot,
I am man's sigh for summer,
the falling leaf of thought.

Was there a time I wonder
when sister-like possessed
and spelled with future sunshine
I thought her dream the best,

one other ghost I loved then
that in my shadows strayed,
a parting kiss I dreamt then
of love's relinquished shade?

—ooOoo—

'The jewel of the north,
to strangers an attraction', so
a dying bishop wrote to his weak king
nights after the king's son set fire to it
and watched with a fierce joy the seeking flame.
Farmers of Elgin would raise croft and dyke
with what the Wolf of Badenoch had left
of blackened stone, the ruins of their church.
And now I come and see it as when whole,
the brave intention thought to be fulfilled,
the jewel that a kingdom sometime wore,
that like itself was lost.

In the remembrance of Simplicity
who once was here, and of the something rare
that visited her ordinary face
with more than ordinary beauty, this
cathedral rose, and in its lift of power,
not less of grace, was greatly simple still,
yet failed its purposed image; she was gone
and missed by the dimension of a smile.
Away and outward spiring yet it spoke
a not quite utter sense of loss;
the sky was all the emptier where it reached.

For all the skills in colour and in sound,
in sculpture and the scarce less durable
designs of fine-wrought wood and pictured glass,
the high-flung vaults and eyeless vacancies
enclosing them, this was no house of man,
and only in such a house would she have dwelt.
Loud as the many choiring centuries
might hymn their faith, silence ruled in this place,
community dispersing down long aisles.
Simplicity that made men saints, at first
wandered in deserts, settled then in towns
gathered her twos and threes, had she stayed here
would best have seen the face she loved so well
with the shut eyes of prayer.

Simplicity looked simply upon death
but here the two keys opened the same door,
always to earth and its dear dignities.
In a dim transept shafted sunshine lights

an armoured tomb, a blizzard of gold dust
bursts on the air, dead bishops still process.
This was a strength of castled Christendom
and fell, of course, like every dream that builds.

—ooOoo—

When I was going someone took
me by the hand and bade me stay
and a long habit of consent
ruled me so that life had his way;
but not life unaccompanied
and of itself could move me so,
it was the insistent face of love
that would not take for answer no.

—ooOoo—

Interior by Vermeer,
peace and order and poise,
light on the dustless air,
only the stillest noise,
a bourgeois, balanced beauty,
thought noble and unfree,
white linen bands of duty
on fine hands' poetry.

A woman at the keys
eliciting the tune
with which her married days
have passed in unison;
paradise has been lost
paradise been regained,
flowers make their lovely boast
from fields the seas profaned.

Thus the puritan soul
measures its days in Leyden,
tastes the sweets of control,
recomposes its Eden,

finds with its faith a home
where life may turn for rest
and death when it will come
come as a decent guest.

—ooOoo—

In the scriptorium
a calm of order dreamt
above the blazoning pen
and gave love's colouring
to scenes that do not fade.
Light falls upon the page
as on the first of days
and never since so bright,
nor ever since a dream
so definite, such life
in the arrested shape,
such will not to let speak
the dissident heart.
Here is the four-walled world,
the pathed and plotted earth;
between its bright-built towers
fair souls like angels walk,
or stand stilled in their talk
like stationary fires.
This world goes by the clock,
its stars are fixed,
it has its Book of Hours
illumined wondrously.
Upon a base of blood
heart-hues are rainbowed out,
from east to west
goes man's endeavour
bright to the setting.
Oh well embroidered that rich night
when, stabled, time left fleeting!
What courage was in man
to wield such colours;

and we in vain record
beggary bedded rich
and folly trumpeted
while these bright shapes keep here
their minstrel summers.

—ooOoo—

A heat-washed afternoon,
a framed and staring town,
a blind dome that looks down
on a life-emptied street
that neither leaves nor enters the still town;
brown cobbles in slow climb,
a slight autumnal cloud
of yellow leaves above a motted wall;
as the last stop of time
a corner's rust-red tiles;
houses close-faced, withdrawn, that keep
in a green-shuttered sleep
their hid inhabitants,
so seeming sound you wonder will they wake
when the first traveller enters the still town.
And yet from every house I hear
the unacknowledged wish, the unuttered sigh,
for the intruder life, the stranger love.
If you should turn that corner and appear
windows would open everywhere,
there would be people in that town;
I should be walking up that street
as you walked down,
and the whole purpose of that town
would be that we should meet.

—ooOoo—

Across the street's bright screen
faces of women flicker,
smile suddenly into the light,
startle the air with colour,

escape from the passing scene
fleetingly;
faces I do not know
and yet I know what they mean,
the many faces of love
that have not been
other than faces to me
till this last summer,
and now are only one
lighted face that I see
lifted into the sun
and smiling seriously.

—ooOoo—

There is a garden green again,
was withered once and once more grows,
and through it listened to by men
once more the quiet river flows.

It is not lost, you still can hear
begin and end, end and begin
the green day's song, and still not fear
illusion from the heart within;

that *will* find order in the wars
of nature and the inchoate heaven,
a love that moves the sun and stars,
a music to their movements given.

The heart within that for a spell
had been so bravely fabulous
is back beside the wishing well
but all its tales are told of us.

No frightened poet that forebodes
an end of all his lying years
and hears approach by many roads
the close pursuer of his fears,

it tells a tale of happiness
just as it knows it might have been,
and as it was, no more, no less,
when two walked in yon garden green.

—ooOoo—

Times there were when it seemed
only a dream within the greater dream
dreamt by the night. Then they went wondering
the ways their loves had gone and come so safe.
In Joyous Garde, and no sword set between
but a sea sundering from her husband king,
Iseult with Tristan lay, and knew again
the moods his cloudy symbols summoned back,
more his than hers, when still they fled and hoped.
    'We wandered south, the sunshine came,
a most uncertain comforter;
all through that season of dismay
we doubted endlessly,
but with the winter we were there
remembering. Weather was variable,
we looked on skies that we had never seen
and could not prophesy;
we could not say into what world we went
and only hoped our feelings had been wise.
At times there fled only the slightest cloud
across a sea-sent sky
and then was happiness,
yet other days disposed us differently.
At length the weathers came to us alone
in our sole season and self-place
out of that other sun;
none but this secret country could afford
a climate to our loving.
But we were so long travelling
and with so many reasons not to arrive
the manner of it can surprise me yet.
I am surprised by you.'
    Darkness knew that she smiled, and Tristan too,
and it was as the moment when they met
and a path opened to their feet
from which there was no turning, and they looked
into a world of common loveliness
where all but feeling slept, and just as then
they entered and came back to given peace;
he to the wonder that was fair Iseult
(sometimes a smile means almost everything),
she to a room, a rightness felt with him,
and a dimension past all others bright
and lightening every scene.

When first she felt his still returning gaze
a fire upon her cheek, and the day dimmed
to flare about her new.
People moved as they'd always moved,
flickeringly, and only they were slow
and singularly real.
That summer had a sky like none since seen,
and woods to walk in now unvisited,
with light and silences about their words;
leaves fell through time so slowly, they made love;
days that no after-days would ever match,
such nights, such mornings too,
birds plucking strings so tentatively tender,
muted preliminaries to orchestral day,
the moment when life sang.
She had not thought the country of lost grace
was waiting to be entered on again.

One curtained hour when to their parent eyes
the night became their child, so vast a love
they tendered, and the same their vow was made:
midsummer flight and no delaying dark,
hedges and trees with flying manes blown by,
the earth a stone struck back and splintering
into the broken colours of the dawn,
always their pace too slow;
till on the sands fallen in each other's arms
morning discovered them,
round them the ring of trampling horse and men,
and the fierce eyes fixed only on the sword,
the lie that saved.

Final escape when an itinerant time
fetching about by many twists and turns
let them remember love, and harboured them:
when they had walked the coloured quays among
watching the quaint-rigged craft put in, their crews
tanned by strange suns, salt winds; seen, where they berthed,
the traders bargaining; heard everywhere
fantastic the downswoop, upswing of gulls
come in their crying crowds bewildering;
at last to purpose found an answering sail.

How good to cease from movement, to be still,
carried to peace,
out where the mornings and the evenings pass
with the same face of journeying happiness,

where sky and sea and ship are endless now,
and elsewhen is a country out of mind,
and now moves on. Time was the simplest thing
when it went with you, as it then had done.
And saddest too was suddenly her thought,
else bliss so much like pain
you closed your eyes on it had not been theirs,
nor Tristan made his verse:
'They come to the magnificence of living
only who love, and whom love does not spare.
Say this of me, and in your castled calm
remember how I sought you stair on stair
and found you in the last withdrawing room,
and held you while our lips remembered there.'
    In Joyous Garde enchantment safely come
knew that it holidayed.

—ooOoo—

Thought
that goes no further than the moonlight falls,
that moves content along the paths of light,
tracing upon the dark a known design,
Orion, the Great Bear, the Pleiades,
almost a shape the silence on the sands,
vanishingly the Mediterranean line,
such thought, that is not thought, is no bad thing
and better than the argument waged here;
from its still centre it takes in the night
as something given and not for questioning.
This way at least I win a quiet heart.

—ooOoo—

Removed from hate as love
the indifferent troops went by,
the still left living men
into the desert sun
and everywhere found life,
even in that emptiness.

It called them out of doors
like children to their play
of guns, though these were real,
or sent them to the shade
of tented rest, or death
crossed, helmeted. So great
a playground in the sun
the desert was.

—ooOoo—

Quiet, quiet, now it is gone,
the herd stampeding, stampeding,
the hard hooves roaring, rearing on top,
light jagging the many-hornèd sky.
Quiet, quiet, now it is gone.

Out of the night comes someone walking,
he has been tired and now he would rest.
Do not heed him, go on with your talking.
There, let him sit down alone, that is best.
The flames on the woodfire are hissing, squawking,
the mother will soon come back to the nest.

It is a bright September morning,
the black birds are flying above the white,
the high sound carries no word of warning,
even as they swoop he is out of the light,
out of the light into the night.

Out of the rock-jagged creek he climbs, the sun
strikes fire from quartz, the sand-glass shakes,
time is running out, no need to run,
he stops, time stops with him;

stops this now light, now dark, dimensioned being,
whose moving is the interchange of worlds,
who shaken is from seeing to unseeing,
who sees again the patterns of light
grow on the day. Or staying now or fleeing
his way is through the night like other men.

—ooOoo—

'I have come back the way I did not want,
from the sweet waters to the bitter town;
we all are ghosts and the wide world we haunt
has but one place in it that makes us real.
My luck it should be this: the grey, grey walls,
the street that never turned a happy face
on the bright sun, the harbour where men watched
an ever lessening sail quite out of sight
as if they went with it; yet this the place
as at day's end from calling open door
fetches its children in, and knows they come.
Home is no word for it, it is myself,
who have no home but just such kind despair.
I went and stayed, travelled to come to this,
all corners turned into the street of fate.
Ithaca is my journey, Ithaca
is all the ports that I shall ever make,
Ithaca that so well can wait.'

—ooOoo—

Let us return to what we once believed:
we enter life as children do their school
with cry and clamour till the hour relieved
(were there such children, was there such a school?)
when none shall call us obdurate or fool;
when none shall say, 'You wicked foolish child,
your lesson is not learned, your work not done,
you'll never learn a thing but to run wild
and vex your father's heart for such a son';
when in that father's arms we shall be home
and in that father's smile know only this,
to him we are not grown-ups fit for blame,
to give a strict account of this and this,
but are forgiven all, so we come home,
and in the end are children, and are his.

—ooOoo—

I am the way, the truth, the life,
I have taken to me a worldly wife
and still she fills my house with strife.
Did I do well?
For now my way is through her land,
my truth what she will understand,
my life in her untender hand,
heaven with hell.

My children will not follow me,
nor her, but in them I shall see
those things in which we both agree.
What things are these?
Only desire to find a way,
only a love that goes astray,
only a truth for a short day,
these things must please.

—ooOoo—

A tippling, toppling world,
buildings of tallest stature, great extent,
are falling with such sober drunkenness
towards the walker in the distant street,
so staid and cheerful in his innocence.
He only knows his city is immense
and takes no hint of imminent descent
from the slow-lengthening shadows at his feet.
Will he reach exit just before it fall,
or stop to buy a paper? Will he learn
about his falling world yet share its fate?
He leaves all questions to the sure event
that's even now answering, so long ago
innoculated by his little death
against for him a no more vast surprise.

—ooOoo—

Here in the highlands is such a patience,
a waiting that is old as are the hills,
so that the silence in which stones are standing
is felt to lean on the companion air,
heavy with time.
 Here is a land not young among time's children
and tall when continents were sea-clad plains,
whose heathered slopes were dark and bright volcanoes,
whose Wood of Calydon marched to the main,
and still roots there.
 Here are proud names that read like battle-honours,
though these now listless hang, their boast now still,
names that the land supports when men turn from them,
that wait the time when the lapsed wind will blow
northward again.
 Here are such heights as overlooking hills
gaze upon lochs that sweep like ships to sea,
and take you with them voyage by questing voyage,
and as you will it take you endlessly,
their dreaming fare.
 Here is a song that is the song of silence
expecting one day an intrusive sound,
but what that sound will be no man imagines,
he only listens, and the hills with him,
the sky, the sea.
 Yes there is movement, miles and miles of it,
murmurous, indistinct, streams seen, unseen,
a shadow-shift and lone wing greatly sailing,
but the tranced watcher only sees himself,
stretched out and still,
one with the land on which he dreams his dream.

—ooOoo—

The tall knight and the hill
high castled in its dream,
the idly pointing spears
above the moveless stream,
the lion banner spread
stiff on the windless air,
all, all so safely still
they will not trouble us,

the thrifty men;
but the dark conjuring
of the daemonic soul,
the undefeated blood,
that is a different thing.
Still it will speak,
still it will come with us,
'I have brought you to the ring.
Dance!'
On the illumined page
the colours faithfully
deployed are banners suddenly
waving above a voice,
and the spears move.

—ooOoo—

My mother loved to listen to the sea,
to sit through afternoons of listening,
as if in the strong wave's so regular fall
she heard a pulse of silence and of peace
beat powerfully, and an immense romance
and mystery speak to her the whole length
of the sea's reach. So great capacity
for peace she had, perhaps as great a need.
She died too by the sea and at the time
of sunset, having said 'How beautiful!',
then cried out with heart's pain. Doubtless the sea
was then as regular in its strong fall
and beat of inborne peace, the even louder skies
just as she said before her listening ceased.

—ooOoo—

When the south wind blows
dust on the bright air flows
and the strayed fancy goes
to no clear end.

When the sirocco blew
and heat was like a dew
on body and mind too
Paolo turned

to Rimini; Francesca sprung
of his own kin, and young
beyond her lord, among
strange folk goes lonely.

He packs the new romance
to read her, idly the old dance
he enters, the cool glance
turns hot, burns deeper.

Love in its privy place
prays from a dreaming face,
'Blow wind, blow wind of grace,
and straight stem bow';

in Rimini's tall tower,
its highest, happiest bower,
reads to the word of power
where reading stops:

'And Lancelot then said
there is in me such dread
of love for you, near dead
I wait your kiss.'

What else romance might tell,
its moment love read well
and the great shadow fell
mocking and tender.

So kind a kiss was there
neither had sense to hear
steps on a secret stair
endlessly nearing.

And still of love the tale
goes on, and the wings sail
on the dun air and pale
haunting together,

going still hand in hand
into the other land
men go for loving, scanned
even in hell.

So these two lives were spent
and doomed by high intent,
but love's diminishment
is all I see,

and how the south wind blows.

—ooOoo—

There is a fire that will consume
and give no pain,
and from its ashes we will spring
Phoenix again;
but no Arabian centuries
are ours to blaze and die,
like stars upon the tree of night
we nest, at dawn we fly.

—ooOoo—

The heavens have a window on our world
thronged with bright faces, all are fools;
the brightest stars are cattle and come near
only to stare and driftingly retreat;
and we are no less unintelligent.
What is it that we do, this fantasy
that so deliberately we prepare.
in which already we participate,
moving towards it with so soft a pace,
as if we circled one another's dream
or moved about each other in a dance
of ceremony? All's pattern, we process
in rituals more ancient than the moon
and with as set a grace. Our destined act
that discreates all reason to create

is distant as a nova; a star went,
and we light-years from what we felt dispersed
know in spent heavens a temporary rest.
Just on the brink of sleep unguessed at loss
disturbs, a great defeat, a god was missed;
somewhen the pattern was passed,
but we were blind and senses burst
into a world not ever meant for us.
Perhaps we should
go to bed only in a dream.

—ooOoo—

Remote
and brilliant as the city of the mind
was the grey chancel, where the white-cold light
from windows shafted beat on death as life
indifferently,
a chapel time might reach but never touch
with an affection, so
the morning showed it, mute and bare.
And yet I found and find you there;
when sunlight on the sainted glass
makes the madonna's smiles caress
the infant Jesus they possess
the beauty of your tenderness,
and time draws near.
    Revealed as empty as its visitor
the haloed altar shone. I came away,
or would have done,
but a stray sunbeam entering the porch
lighted the Virgin in her shadowed niche
and tricked her in the semblance of your smile.
I stayed to pray,
and spoke the blasphemy not felt as such,
I prayed to you:
in the retreat and convent of your grace
there to remember me,
who set religion wholly in your face,
who would not see
the cross except depending from your neck,
and childed there

44

in the close sanctuary of your breast,
where all the love and faith I'd ever known
had found their rest.
I spoke your name
and all the congregated centuries
joined in my prayer, always the same.
Paris again praised Helen in a church,
and in a church proud Troilus' idle search
stopped upon Cressid's face;
mine stopped on yours and it seemed right to pray,
for I had found my image, where alone
my wish was to be heard.

—ooOoo—

Your head was on my shoulder when I thought
'How still she makes my world'; and this was not
in a room's spreading quiet but a packed train
racing as if its iron heart must strain
and burst for many travellers,
and yet we were its only passengers.
You slept and my arm did not move at all,
our journey through the evening had become
perpetual.
What stops were made, what stations we passed through,
were names that came and went, seen fleetingly
and given no heed. We had a destination
but as it seemed to me we had arrived.
Another train than that we travelled in
went its companion journey through the night,
dark stops and stations it would have to pass
for that continuing moment out of mind.

—ooOoo—

'Be very careful how you dream,
the nights are long in passing',
said to me that great dreamer day
when much too late for listening.

'You will meet faces in the night
I never dreamt for you,
and they will smile at you and go
their unremembering way.

But sometimes one will stay for you
clear as when it was dreamt
and I will share with you your dream
through all the long daylight.'

As he had said night brought its dream
to share it with the day,
and the strange face I looked upon
was known and went its way.

—ooOoo—

You showed me daffodils,
and on the wind-stopped hills in streaks
the lingering snows,
and spring scarce kind upon the trees,
and the small count of cottages
a scant earth spared,
an abbey, distanced inconceivably
from our concerns
but where you checked my instant sacrilege,
still speculating from its random stones,
above a dense-dark stream hyaena's den,
you read me runes in a cold church.
All are commingled now,
the ermined daffodils,
the flowing dark on which a wild beast laughs,
the runic cold and the discouraging church,
as features of a day undifferenced
by any stint of love, residual care.
Random and cold as were your abbey stones
are now my memories, distinct and vague,
a frustrate day with all events so clear
but not the face above the daffodils.

—ooOoo—

So many different kinds of loving,
hopeful and hurtful every one,
and the beauty making a heart's wonder
not that they end but that they are begun,
for a dimension entered, never left,
that countervails all pain.
I look, too much aware
of idle hands that stroke
a memory of your hair,
at something marvellous.
Do buildings cry when they fall down
that have been lived in?
It is imaginable,
as also that they shimmer still
almost substantial in the exploded air.
Beauty is a continuing property,
and I can be hurt another day
as willingly.

—ooOoo—

Once from her mind there played a lute,
music so clear and undesigned
as if just wandering by the way
the tune was there for her to find.

Or that was how it seemed to me
when first I knew her, worlds ago;
she talked, I listened, the voice flowed,
the sound was all I cared to know.

I do not listen now for sound,
only for sense, the voice goes on;
I did not know how much it meant
until the music all was gone.

And yet a music worlds away
and listened to, when silence fall
can still be heard, its seeming end
not altogether terminal.

—ooOoo—

There is a tale of folly having come
to a clear water, where he stayed to see
the shape of life come to him as himself,
and in that self was lost. For there he saw
ideal love returned, no face shut fast
against the recognition of its kind,
nor kindness mirrored where no kindness was
but a smile wholly given as was his own,
and still the help where there was need of it,
and the whole world seen as a dreamer's well.
So long he looked evening still found him there,
and growing dark, the stars shone back more bright,
the pale face pleaded, the smile almost gone;
'I come, I come', he cried, and the night saw
the faint white circles made. His name is kept,
lovely and always sad, in a lone flower
white as those circles were. Perhaps none flee
that fate of folly in his imaged world
who give themselves to words; or there are some
make for the green banks laughing, nothing seen
of love's lost face; or yet more wise, more few,
that seek for language as a stone to drop
into a quiet pool whose ripples spread
past instant thought and feeling to find bed
in undemanding peace. Such fugitives
may fashion beauty in their hurtless kind;
and yet that wildflower, by the margin grows
and memory tends, their dreaming fellow left,
who would wish quite away?

—ooOoo—